Online Money Making Businesses

www.vojemfortune.com

Introduction

The internet has made possible ways to make money online in legitimate ways you can ever imagine. It takes sheer determination on your part to make something out of it.

Can you make money online? Yes. Is it easy? No. Can I be scammed if I choose the wrong ones? Yes. In this e-book, you will learn some wonderful ways to make money online legitimately and not worry about being scammed.

For starters, you should create a website/blog. This will be your online presence to connect with all your businesses. Many businesses wont take you serious if you don't have a blog.

Online Businesses You Can Do With Your Website/Blog

1. You can create a search engine .
2. Start a social media and forum.
3. Start video streaming website.
4. Start a job website or job search engine.
5. Start an online store.
6. Create an affiliate shop.
7. Start an entertainment blog.

www.vojemfortune.com

8. Start an information resource blog.

9. Start a news website.

10. Create a soccer analysis blog.

11. Start a free classified website.

12. Start a directory website.

13. Create a tech blog.

14. Start a music download website.

15. Start a food blog.

16. Start a freelance website.

17. Start an information marketing website.

18. Affiliate marketing

19. Website and domain flipping.

20. Bulk sms website.

21. Web design website.

CHAPTER ONE

Blogging

Blogging is all about creating a blog and writing on a specific niche of your passion. You can write on health, weight loss, fashion, tech, sports and any niche of interest.

Creating your site and monetizing it is the way to go. Let us look at the ways you can monetize your blog.

Make money from your blog in the following ways.

Generate traffic and sell affiliate products.

Host paid webinars

Allow sponsored posts on your blog.

Allow Paid advertisement on your blog through sites like buysellads, bidvertiser, anonymous ads.

Place ads from ad networks on your site like google adsense, infolinks, media.net, chitika, revenuehits

Sell digital products with woocommerce on your wordpress blog or with shopify on both wordpress or blogger blog.

Start a paid directory on your site.

www.vojemfortune.com

Chapter Two

Generate Steady Income With Google Adsense

Do you have a site or a blog, if yes, then it is good for you to apply and place Google adsense on your site/blog. If you don't have a blog create one to benefit as other bloggers do from ad advertisement.

Google Adsense has become the most important and easy way to make money online by bloggers. Just placing the ad codes on your blog is the magic step towards a steady stream of income if and only if you are approved by Google Adsense.

Google Adsense is a thing of joy to many bloggers in today's world of blogging. Making money through ads placed by Adsense on your blog is money making generator of sort.

In this post, I will show you steps to take before applying for Google Adsense and steps to take after getting approval to increase your Google Adsense revenue.

Steps To take Before Applying For Google Adsense

Get a domain name and hosting plan.

Create a blog of a good niche such as entertainment, fashion, tech.

Give your blog a good design

Get SEO friendly template.

Ensure to put the following on your navigation menu such as About Us, Contact Us, Terms and Conditions, Privacy Policy, Label/Categories, Blog Archives, Author Profile, Sitemap.

Ensure to fill your blog with unique and original content.

Let the content be more than 350 words per post.

Before applying for Google Adsense, ensure you have at least 25 original posts.

Your posts must be unique and original from you and informative to your readers.

After creating your blog ensure to post regularly.

Make use of the following SEO methods to drive traffic to your blog such as pinging, social media, blog directories, free classified ads, article directories, PR, forums and social bookmarking.

Ensure to make use of the following on your blog Google Analytics, Google Webmaster Tools(Google Search Console) and Google Tag Manager.

Ensure to fill your content with rich longtail keywords.

Make use of the following to enrich your keyword selection such as Google Keyword Planner, Majesticseo, Moz, Semrush, Keyword.io, and Keyword Advisor Pro.

Ensure your blog is verified with Google Webmaster Tools.

For credibility ensure you have backlinks (inbound links).

Interlink your posts.

Ensure you don't have broken links on your blog. This is very important.

To avoid this, make use of linkminer and broken link checker.

Make use of Pagespeed to check your site's loading speed.

Use www.website.grader.com to analyze your blog.

Get royalty free pictures for your blog such as flickr and pixabay.

Social media sharing buttons are very important. Place them on your blog to promote sharing of your posts.

Make use of Updates to update your posts regularly.

Submit your blog to search engines such as Google, Bing, Entireweb and Yahoo.

www.vojemfortune.com

Chapter Three

Income Generating Websites For Writers And Publishers

These websites discussed below are money making sites for writers, authors and publishers. They are specially created for publishers, authors, writers and bloggers to make extra money.

Making money online is the essence of online businesses. Ad networks, affiliate marketing, blogging, online advertising all projects money making ventures .

In view of this, many websites owners has deviced many forms of making money online. Sites now render a kind of service you register to engage in and get paid to do some kind of tasks.

In this post, I will show 20 legitimate websites that pays you for doing little tasks.

20 Legitimating Money Paying Websites

Hubpages

For Who: Freelance writers and Publishers

Mode Of Payment: Paypal

Minimum Payout: Hubpages $50, Google Adsense $100

Info: Articles published on hubpages can be monetized with google adsense, hubpages ad programs, amazon and ebay affiliate websites. You will receive commissions for every product sold through your affiliate links.

Funds For Writers

For Who: Original content writers

Info: You are paid when your articles get published

www.vojemfortune.com

Link From Blog

For Who: Writers and Publishers

Info: They don't charge any commission from publishers earnings

Wisebread.com

For Who: Writers

Info: They accept articles on personal finance topics, 3 samples of work demanded and revenue sharing that comes articles submitted.

Revenue Stream

For Who: Review writers or Publishers

Info: $1.50 or more per submitted reviews. Submitted reviews must not be published on your blog.

Epinions.com

For Who: Review writers and Publishers

Info: Accepts reviews of at 20 words and allows articles to be published on your site.

The bloggers Network

For Who: Writers and Publishers

www.vojemfortune.com

Info: Monetizes your articles and 0% commissions. Services render are desktop displayed ads, native ads, interstitial ads, mobile specific display ads, rich media ads, in-image and in-screen ads.

Payperpost

For Who: Writers and Publishers

Info: Pays for every published reviews on their blog. Requirements include, 3 months old blog, high page rank, 20 quality posts and in English language.

Sponsoredreviews

For Who: Advertisers and Publishers

Info: Requirements includes 3 month old blog, indexed in major search engines and 10 high quality posts for publishers. For advertisers, they help them generate more traffic from search engines.

Digitaljournal.com

For Who: Writers and Publishers

Mode Of Payment: Paypal

Minimum Payout: $10

Info: You get paid for reporting original news and writing news items for the site.

Social Spark

For Who: Writers and Publishers

Info: You are required to write reviews articles advertisers products and services on your blog.

PayU2blog

For Who: Writers and Publishers

Info: They advertise on your blog and pay every two weeks but your blog must be above 3 months old.

Worldstart

For Who: Tech writers and publishers

Mode Of Payment: 400 words $20, 600 words $30, and 800 words $35

Info: Submitted images and articles must be unique and original.

Make A Living Writing

For Who: Writers and Publishers

Info: $75-$100 per post selected. Articles must be detailed and of good quality.

Linkworth

For Who: Advertisers and Publishers

Info: They buy and sell text links and paid reviews on blogs. Publishers earns extra money by sending advertisers to their sites.

SeedingUp

For Who: Advertisers and Publishers

Info: They sell paid reviews for advertisers written by publishers. They also sell text links.

Software Judge

For Who: Writers and Publishers

Payout: $50

Info: As a writer, you write reviews on the software available on the site.

www.vojemfortune.com

Listverse

For Who: Writers and Publishers

Payout: $100 per article

Info: Top news magazine covering variety of topics. Submitted articles must be unique and over 1500 words.

Blogvertise

For Who: Writers and Publishers

Info: Best blog required for approval. At least 3 links allowed in written reviews to advertisers websites. Submitted reviews must be more than 100 words and completed within 5 days.

Chapter Four

Paid Survey

Making money online has become the in thing now. Creating a blog, being involved in affiliate marketing or PPC is all about making money. In this post, I will show you how to make money from legitimate paid surveys.

Many thinks paid surveys are waste of time but at the end of reading this post, you will be glad you did. This post will make paid surveys an interesting way to make money online for you.

Benefits Of Paid Surveys

When you register, you will start making money instantly.

You don't need any special skill

No investment needed

You are allowed to take the surveys at your own pace and convenience

Tips For Paid Surveys

Register a new e-mail address

Make sure you have a Paypal and Payoneer accounts

Make sure you can receive their e-mail communications

The under listed paid surveys are tested and proven survey panels. Just register with any one of them and start making money immediately.

www.vojemfortune.com

Lists Of Legitimate Paid Survey

GlobalTestMarket

Payment Type   Paypal, Checks and Cards

Minimum Payout $20

Services   Mobile surveys

iPoll

Payment Type   Paypal, Retail vouchers

Minimum Payout $50

Services   Mobile surveys, Product Reviews

Pinecone Research

Payment Type   Paypal and Check

Minimum Payout $3

Services   Mobile surveys and Product Reviews

Fusioncash

Payment Type   Paypal and Bank Transfer

Minimum Payout $25

Services   Paid to watch videos, paid to shop, paid web search, paid sign up

www.vojemfortune.com

VIP Voice

Payment Type   Gift, cash and sweepstakes

Minimum Payout $20

Services   Instant win games and focus groups

Toluna

Payment Type   Paypal, Gift card and Check

Minimum Payout $20

Services   Mobile surveys and Product reviews

OpinionOutpost

Payment Type   Paypal

Minimum Payout $50

Services   Mobile Surveys

Harris Poll Online

Payment Type   Gift Cards

Minimum Payout   100 points

Services   Mobile Surveys

www.vojemfortune.com

iSay By Ipsos

Payment Type   Paypal, Cash and Gift Cards

Minimum Payout $10

Services   Mobile Surveys and Product reviews

Inboxdollars

Payment Type   Visa card, Cash and Check

Minimum Payout $30

Services   Daily Surveys

Swagbucks

Payment Type   Paypal and Gift Cards

Minimum Payout $5

Services   Paid games, Mobile surveys and Paid to serach

ShoppingJobs.com

Payment Type   Paypal

Minimum Payout $50

Services   Mystery shopping and product Reviews

Nielsen Digital Voice

Payment Type   Sweepstakes

Minimum Payout $50

Services   Mobile Surveys

Vindale Research

Payment Type   Paypal

Minimum Payout $50

Services   Product Reviews

Mysurvey

Payment Type   Paypal and Sweepstakes

Minimum Payout $50

Services   Mobile Surveys, Webcam Surveys and Products Reviews

Chapter Five

PTC

Hello friends, want to know how to make thousands of dollars from PTC? Paid To Click sites gives out cents per click on adverts on their sites. You can make a couple of hundreds of dollars from this scheme if you are serious.

At first, it might be discouraging as the cents might not result to something tangible in the beginning, don't worry, in this post we are going to discuss ways to gather a huge from these cents resulting to thousands of dollars in a month.

STEP 1
Register with these Payment processors:

https://perfectmoney.is/?ref=5524895

STEP2
Register with the following sites. Click on the links and start making money

<a href="http://www.clixsense.com/?9652123" target=_blank><img src="http://csstatic.com/banners/clixsense468x60a.gif" border=0></a>

https://www.neobux.com/?r=godwinstar2004□

http://clixten.info/?ref=godwinstar2004

http://www.grandclick.com/?ref=godwinstar2004

http://www.ultimateclixx.com/?ref=godwinstar2004

www.vojemfortune.com

http://europrofit.tk/?ref=godwinstar2004

http://www.twickerz.com/?ref=godwinstar2004

http://www.silverclix.com/?ref=godwinstar2004

http://buxvertise.com/?ref=godwinstar2004

http://www.goldenclix.com/?ref=godwinstar2004

When you have registered with all these PTC websites, you login and click on the ads available on them for the day. You can also make more money by clicking on offers and surveys and doing all the jobs given you

The little secret to making more money on PTC is doing the following:

1. Use adverts of your referral link to win more people to the PTC sites that you are registered with.
2. You can place your referral link on your website, blog, facebook, twitter etc
3. You can also rent refferals from the PTC sites you are registered with. The more your rented referrals clicks, the more money you make.

www.vojemfortune.com

Chapter Six

Social Media Marketing

Sell affiliate products on your social media handles. One of the fastest way to sell your products is through social media

Facebook

Promote your products and services 6 times a day or more.

Sell membership to your facebook group.

Create a store on your facebbook page

Place facebook ads to sell your products and services.

Set up a custom audience that has visted your site before for retargeting.

Place a call to action in your page picture

How To Make Money From Instagram

Create an account

Post regularly

Take good photos

Use relevant hashtags

Use tagforlikes app

Engage with your followers.

www.vojemfortune.com

Instagram Affiliate Marketing

Post attractive images highlighting their products and drive sales through your affiliate URL.

Affiliates- sharesale, ebates, stylinity.

Use bitly.com to shorten and customize your affiliate link.

Create sponsored posts.

Use tapinfluence.

Use Ifluenz.

Sell your photos to twenty20 and community foap.

Promote your business , products and services.

Use Repost for instagram.

Use Infographics plus exclusive offers

Sell your instagram account to fameswap and viral accounts.

Connect with companies- quglu, quickshouts, popular pays, takumi app, snapfluence, instabrand.

How To Make Money Online From Twitter

Create a twitter account if you don't have one.

Register with kwerdo.com to get affiliate links to post on twitter.

Get more followers by following everyone and anyone in the niche you are promoting.

Use sponsoredtweets through ad.ly, magpie, twitpub or twittad.

Use mylikes, ad.ly, revtwt, twittad, paidtweets.

www.vojemfortune.com

To get followers on twitter type "followback","follow me","follow for follow","F4F".

Follow anyone and everyone who follows the biggest followback networks.

Follow 200 per day without getting into trouble.

Trending: See what is trending and check what's got the most re-tweets and then just copy what they have said on your twitter. Change it into your own words and do it twice a day.

Tags: Tag 2 posts on things people look at. Look at trends and only tag when I'm posting about trending topics.

Create A Good Twitter Profile

Profile, use (Avatar + Bio)

Use logo nerds

Celebrity followers. Get them to follow you by following them.

Chat with someone. Click on discover and chat with someone of your interest.

Go to trending topics and talk to people there.

Get a twitter queue bot.

Rant. Use a vine and some angry caption text.

Create content with pictures, vines and posts.

NOTE: After creating a good twitter account, get many followers especially the celebrity followers. Ensure to put your affiliate links in every of your posts. Posts regularly and watch your earnings grow. Happy twitting!!!

www.vojemfortune.com

How To Make Money From Tumblr

Create a tumblr account with professional touch.

Register with infolinks, chitika, kontera, viglink, ebates, linkshare to get adverts displayed on your tumblr account and blog.

Pay for uploaded files- rapidgator or depositfiles.

Adding URL or link to other files e.g adf.ly, shorte.st, linkshrink.net.

Upload pictures e.g imagetwist,imagecherry

Use tumblrjazz, an automated way to get followers on tumblr

Use Queue+ to load 2000 images. Set to function for 20 days.

Load up blog

Get chrome extension Archive poster

Go to niche tumblr, URL and add "archive"

Then click "select" and select photos

Then click "Post" and "Queue+"

Go back to Queue+ and set a schedule

The posts are set to run.

Get woozone from wordpress.

Create a good hosted website.

To make on tumblr, go to queue+, click on tumblr blog profile and click edit all post. Put the URL to the website in the caption.

NOTE: You make money from tumblr by the adverts placed on your blog through it with chitika, kontera, viglinks etc.

www.vojemfortune.com

How To Make Money From Google+

Create a google+ account.

Add target subscribers of your niche of interest.

Create a page in google+ profile about tab.

Include affiliate links of your choice.

Run google+ hangouts.

Create a community. Create your page with a name of your product, also add on "About the product" details

Create a cover pic

Sell your product in your google+ community.

Promote books. Your ebooks or of others.

Increase affiliate products especially in every post

Offer services like freelancing, web design, consulting etc.

Create a blog dedicated to google+

NOTE: You make your money by the affiliate links you post and services you offer.

How To Make Money From Youtube

Create a youtube account.

Know the type of video you want to upload.

Enable monetization and sign up for google adsense.

Become a youtube partner.

Upload content.

www.vojemfortune.com

Upload regularly.

Tag your videos with keywords that describe the content.

Gain audience by sending videos out to twitter and facebook, share with people , distribute elsewhere on the internet. Let us go over it once again:

Sign up for Google and setup your own channel.

Buy HD camera and microphone or use your phone.

Get your video and edit it then upload on YouTube.

Add affiliate links to your videos or get brand offers from sites like ifabbo, massive sway, business2blogger

Advertise on Facebook, Twitter, Reddit, and etc. Use SEO for title search.

Chapter seven

AD Networks

You can make easy money from ad networks. As a blogger, all it takes is for you to register with the highest paying ad network preferably two of them and place their ads on your blog.

The amount they pay per click (CPC) or per impression (CPM) is different. Check them one by one to choose a better one that befits your program and place their ads on your blog.

Register with them, get their approval and place their ads code on your blog. Ads will be served automatically on your blog. Below are some of the ad networks you can register with.

List Of Ad Networks.

Sovr

Facebook Audience Network

Taboola

Propeller Ads

Anonymous Ad

Popads

Buyandsellads

Adblade

OpenX

Viglink

Chitika

Defy Media

Publicity clerks

Adversal

Criteo

Ref Content

Shareasale

Bidvertiser

Clicksor

Brealtime

Adcash

Yesadvertising

Outbrain

Advertising.com

Media.net

DistrictM

Maxbounty

Infolinks

RevenueHits

Qatabra

UberCPM

Conversant

152Media

Asteria Network

Adsoptimal

Google Adsense

Create as many sites or blogs as possible and place these ad networks' codes on your blogs. Ad networks pays per click or per 1000 impression. If you happen to have tens of thousands of traffic you will make some thousands of dollars.

Register with as many ad networks you can and place their ads on your site. Generate enough traffic and make decent extra cash for yourself.

Chapter Eight

Affiliate Marketing

Affiliate marketing is an art of selling someone's products for a commission.

Sign up for the amazon affiliate program, JVZoo, clickbank, CJ affiliate, shareasale.

Get your affiliate links from these pay per action sites and make extra cash whenever a customer make a purchase.

Do Youtube videos and include an affiliate link.

Affiliate marketing is another good way to make extra income online. It is a better alternative to ad networks. Affiliate marketing programs make it easy and profitable for bloggers to earn a decent income on a monthly basis. As a blogger, you can enroll in as much as 5 affiliate programs and post your affiliate links in your posts or pages to start earning a commission.

Earning commissions does not come easy but patience and hard work will bring good result at the end. You can promote your affiliate links with Youtube videos shared in your social media handles like facebook, twitter, LinkedIn, Instagram and Pinterest. Your making money from this program depends on the method you apply.

Check the following affiliate programs and choose the one(s) that suits you.

1. Amazon Associates

2. Clickbank

3. Shareasale

4. Maxbounty

5. E-junkie

6. Ebay affiliate Program

7. Linkshare

8. Pepperjam Network.com

9. CJ.com

10. JVZoo.com

11. Neverblue

12. Clickbooth

13. Peerfly

Ways To Make $100-$200 Daily Via Affiliate Marketing

1. Create a blog with a minimum of 500 traffic views per day. This can be achieved by writing unique content, longtail keywords and use of SEO.

2. Gain your reader's attention by creating an attractive and free e-book for your blog to grow your email list.

3. Always make use of an email autoresponder such as madmini, mailchimp, aweber, or getresponse for your blog.

4. Create a seminar or course on your blog teaching your readers tricks and tips in your niche.

5. Create captivating headlines for your blog.

6. During the seminar or course, endeavor to promote goods and services related to your niche.

7. The winning formula to generate more money is by getting more traffic and email subscribers.

8. Get more traffic by guest posting and commenting on other blogs of your niche.

9. Make use of Youtube videos you created to enhance your affiliate links promotion on social media and anywhere on the web.

10. Get good product links from your affiliate programs to promote to your visitors on your blog and social media.

11. Always ensure that your affiliate links are placed on your posts, pages, social media and anywhere on the web that matters.

12. Always send email messages with good information to your email subscribers with your affiliate links included in the message. Give your email subscribers genuine offers.

Making use of the above list will surely expose your affiliate links to as many visitors as possible and guaranteeing sales worth $100-$200 daily.

www.vojemfortune.com

Chapter Nine

Create And Sell Digital Products

One of the quickest and safest way to make money online is to create your own digital product for sale. What type of skill do you possess that you can sell digitally think about it.

There are many digital products you can create to solve the problems of your customers. Let us take a look at some of them.

List of Digital Products You Can Create.

1. Write ebooks- amazon, createspace, lulu, gumroad, smashwords, kobo.
2. Create an email training course
3. Create a video training course
4. Create graphics or clipart to sell.
5. Build an app or software to sell.
6. Take wonderful photos and sell them on istockphoto and bigstockphoto.
7. Create and sell audio form of your ebooks with programs like ACX
8. Create a digital magazine and sell ads.
9. Create small printables like planner pages, patterns and stickers for sell.
10. Create and sell your custom artwork through digital download, etsy or shopify.
11. Create workbook of systems and forms of different businesses for sale.
12. Create fancy funnel for sale.

Where To Sell Your Digital Products.

Sell on your site or blog.

Sell on Etsy, gumroad and shopify.

Sell on your social media accounts

www.vojemfortune.com

Advertise on free classified ads sites

Sell on your own online store

Sell on marketplaces like Amazon.com, Ebay, shareasale.

Make use of Paypal buttons .

www.vojemfortune.com

Chapter Ten

Make Money From Bitcoins

Bitcoins have come of age. It is used as a form money for business and payments. You can buy and sell in some major online market places in bitcoins. It is not a physical form of money to be handled or counted. That is why it is referred to as crypto currency.

How important or valuable is this crypto currency? At the time of writing, 1 Bitcoin is equivalent to $995. Assuming you have 10 bitcoins, it means you are $9950 richer. Engaging in any business that involves bitcoins will surely enrich you if done properly.

Then how do you benefit from bitcoins? How do you get your own bitcoins? Let us look at the various ways to accumulate bitcoins.

1. Running A Bitcoin Faucet. You can make anywhere between $50-$800 monthly.
   Creating and running a bitcoin faucet is simple.
   You give visitors to your bitcoin faucet some bitcoins for visiting your faucet and doing some micro tasks.

2. Create And Run An Information Blog On bitcoins And Monetize It With Google Adsense. Create a blog that contains information on bitcoins and its benefits. Apply for Google adsense or any good ad network on your site for passive income.

3. Earn Bitcoins By Doing Micro Tasks. There are many websites or faucets out there that are ready to pay you in bitcoins for visiting their sites and completing micro jobs like watching videos, completing surveys, solving recapthas.

www.vojemfortune.com

4. Turn Your Writing Skills To Cash. On the web, there are websites that needs content for their blog. There are others that need reviews for their products. You can write content for them or make reviews on their product on your site and you get paid in bitcoins.

5. Sell Products And Services And Get Paid In Bitcoins. As the owner of your website, you can sell any product or services to the world and receive payment in bitcoins. The all digital currency makes it easy to buy and sell in bitcoins. Receiving payments in bitcoins can never be too easy. Advertise your goods and services both online and offline and place bitcoin payment processor on your site to start receiving payments in bitcoins.

6. Engage In Bitcoin Mining. You mine for bitcoins by solving complex algorithms that create blocks that are added to the public ledger. This ledger is the history of all transactions conducted through bitcoin. Join a bitcoin mining pool today and making money from bitcoin.

7. Buy And Sell Bitcoin. Buy bitcoin today at the current price and sell tomorrow at a higher price for profit. Bitcoin is tightly regulated by the algorithms themselves making the value of bitcoins to increase by the day. Buying bitcoin and selling later for a profit is a good option.

8. Lend Your Bitcoins For A profit. You loan your bitcoins for profit. The risk involved determines the interest rate. Loan with colaterral means low interest rate. Loan without collateral results to high interest rate. Their websites that render services of standing as a go between for lenders and borrowers.

Resources

Learn How to make money from social media ... http://amzn.to/2sNKCtF